Dedication

This book is dedicated to all the individuals, entrepreneurs, and leaders who believe in the power of purpose-driven business to create a better world.

To the visionary trailblazers who have dared to challenge the status quo, who have chosen to put people and the planet at the forefront of their endeavors.

To the tireless advocates who have fought for a more sustainable and equitable future, who have shown us that profit and purpose can coexist harmoniously.

To the employees who have embraced their roles as change agents within their organizations, who have demonstrated that individual actions can have a collective impact.

To the communities and societies that have come together to demand a new paradigm, where businesses prioritize social responsibility and environmental stewardship.

To the mentors and guides who have shared their wisdom and experiences, who have inspired and empowered others to embark on their purpose-driven journeys.

To the next generation of leaders, entrepreneurs, and change-makers who will carry the torch forward and continue to shape a purpose-driven future.

THE PURPOSE-DRIVEN BUSINESS

HOW TO SUCCEED IN THE 21ST CENTURY BY PUTTING PEOPLE AND PLANET FIRST

DR. YOGENDRA SINGH YADAV

Contents

Contents

About The Author

Dr. Yogendra Singh Yadav, hailing from Kanpur, Uttar Pradesh, is a shining example of unwavering dedication to ethics in both life and business. Throughout his remarkable journey, he has consistently demonstrated a commitment to ethical principles, resulting in resounding success in every endeavor he has undertaken. His unyielding integrity has transformed everything he touches into gold.

With a Postgraduate Diploma in Marketing and Sales Management under his belt, Dr. Yogendra Singh Yadav chose to carry on the family bead business, becoming a major supplier of glass beads to bead exporters across the nation. As his expertise and experience in the bead business flourished, he ventured into direct export operations in the early 2000s, swiftly ascending to become a prominent exporter in his city. His products reached far and wide, leaving a trail of satisfied customers and propelling him to new heights.

While pursuing his export business, Dr. Yadav nurtured a deep desire to contribute to the welfare of people in rural villages. Observing that many villagers still employed traditional methods of creating and marketing their wares, such as using chalk for pottery, he felt compelled to help them improve their livelihoods. With his ingenuity, he designed various machines powered by electricity to assist these artisans. His ideas quickly gained popularity, and the government extended support, enabling him to develop more machines that enhanced the living conditions of rural communities.

Having earned acclaim, recognition, and wealth through his unwavering commitment to sincere and ethical work practices, Dr. Yogendra Singh Yadav reached the pinnacle of success. At that point, he made the decision to embark on a research endeavor focused on "How to Succeed in the 21st Century by Putting People and Planet First," a mission that resonates with the entire world. This book is the culmination of his dedicated research work on "The Purpose-Driven Business: How to Succeed in the 21st Century by Putting People and Planet First."

Dr. Yadav's extensive experience in business, his genuine concern for people's well-being, and his deep-rooted commitment to social responsibility make him a true authority on the subject. His insights, wisdom, and practical strategies are distilled within these pages, offering readers invaluable guidance on how to navigate the challenges of the modern era while prioritizing the welfare of both individuals and the environment. Dr. Yogendra Singh Yadav's relentless pursuit of purpose-driven success serves as an inspiration for aspiring entrepreneurs and leaders who seek to create a positive impact on the world.

As a respected thought leader, entrepreneur, and philanthropist, Dr. Yadav continues to inspire others through his actions, embodying the principles he espouses. With his remarkable journey and unwavering dedication to ethical business practices and social responsibility, he leaves an indelible mark on the business world and serves as a guiding light for those who wish to forge their own purpose-driven path.

ϼϼϼ

Preface

In a world where the impact of business extends far beyond the bottom line, the need for purpose-driven organizations has never been more crucial. This book is a guide for individuals, entrepreneurs, and leaders who believe in the power of business to create positive change and are ready to embark on a purpose-driven journey.

The 21st century has brought forth numerous challenges, from social inequality and environmental degradation to ethical dilemmas and shifting consumer expectations. As the world grapples with these complex issues, it has become evident that traditional business models are no longer sufficient. Today's businesses must embrace a broader purpose, one that goes beyond profit and encompasses the well-being of people and the planet.

"The Purpose-Driven Business" is a testament to the belief that businesses can be a force for good. It explores the principles, strategies, and practices that enable organizations to succeed while creating meaningful impact. Through the pages of this book, we will dive deep into topics such as defining purpose, building a purpose-driven culture, sustainable practices, stakeholder engagement, innovation, leadership, and more.

Each chapter offers valuable insights, practical advice, and real-world examples from purpose-driven entrepreneurs and leaders who have navigated the challenges and experienced the rewards of putting people and the planet first. Their stories inspire us to take action, to challenge the status quo, and to reimagine the role of business in society.

"The Purpose-Driven Business" is a call to action—a call for individuals, businesses, and society to come together and build a future that prioritizes purpose, sustainability, and social responsibility. It is an invitation to reflect on our values, to embrace our role as change agents, and to create a positive impact in our own spheres of influence.

As the author of this book, I believe that every business, regardless of size or industry, has the potential to be purpose-driven. Whether you are an aspiring entrepreneur, a seasoned executive, or an employee looking to make a difference, this book provides the tools and insights you need to embark on or further your purpose-driven journey.

I encourage you to approach this book with an open mind and a willingness to challenge conventional wisdom. As you read each chapter, consider how the concepts and strategies apply to your own circumstances. Reflect on the potential for your organization to contribute to a better world, both internally and externally.

"The Purpose-Driven Business" is not just a theoretical exploration—it is a practical guide to creating positive change. It offers actionable steps, thought-provoking questions, and exercises to help you apply the concepts and strategies to your own context.

I hope that this book serves as a source of inspiration, guidance, and empowerment as you embark on your purpose-driven journey. Together, we can shape a future where businesses thrive, people flourish, and the planet thrives. Let us take this transformative journey together and create a purpose-driven world.

Dr. Yogendra Singh Yadav
26-MIG, Indira Nagar, Kanpur-26 (Uttar Pradesh - India)

ﭘﭘﭘ

Disclaimer

"The views expressed in this book are solely those of the author and do not reflect the opinions of any organization or individual. The author respects the right to freedom of speech and expression guaranteed by Article 19(1)(a) of the Constitution of India."

❦❦❦

**The Changing Landscape
A New Era for Business**

*The rise of conscious consumerism and the need for purpose-driven
businesses
The shifting expectations of stakeholders in the 21st century
The economic and social benefits of putting people and planet first*

ᗡᗡᗡ

ONE

The Changing Landscape: A New Era for Business

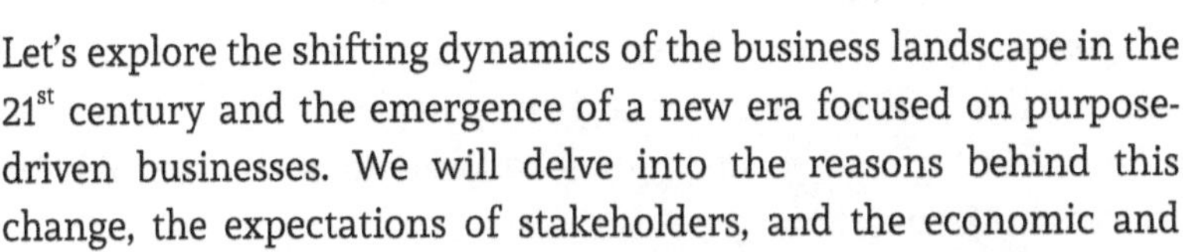

Let's explore the shifting dynamics of the business landscape in the 21st century and the emergence of a new era focused on purpose-driven businesses. We will delve into the reasons behind this change, the expectations of stakeholders, and the economic and social benefits that come with putting people and planet first.

1.1 The Rise of Conscious Consumerism:

In recent years, there has been a notable increase in conscious consumerism. Consumers are becoming more mindful of the social and environmental impact of their purchasing decisions. They demand products and services that align with their values and support causes they care about. This shift in consumer behavior has forced businesses to re-evaluate their practices and prioritize purpose over profit.

1.2 The Need for Purpose-Driven Businesses:

Businesses are no longer solely judged by their financial performance; they are increasingly scrutinized for their impact on society and the environment. Shareholders, customers, employees, and even regulators expect businesses to be responsible and contribute positively to the world. Purpose-driven businesses, which prioritize social and environmental goals alongside financial success, are better positioned to meet these expectations.

1.3 Expectations of Stakeholders:

Stakeholders play a crucial role in shaping the landscape of business. Shareholders now consider environmental, social, and governance (ESG) factors when evaluating investments. Customers seek brands that align with their values and make a positive impact. Employees are increasingly drawn to companies that prioritize purpose and offer meaningful work. Governments and regulators are enacting policies that encourage responsible business practices. Understanding and meeting these expectations is essential for success in the new era.

1.4 The Economic and Social Benefits:

Contrary to conventional belief, purpose-driven businesses can achieve both financial success and social impact. By integrating purpose into their core strategies, these businesses attract and retain loyal customers who support their mission. They also foster a motivated and engaged workforce, leading to increased productivity and innovation. Purpose-driven companies often enjoy long-term sustainability, as they adapt to changing societal needs and mitigate risks associated with environmental and social challenges.

1.5 Embracing the Shift:

To thrive in the new era, businesses must embrace the shift towards purpose-driven practices. This requires a fundamental change in mindset, where profit is not the sole measure of success. It entails aligning values and mission, engaging stakeholders effectively, and adopting sustainable practices. By putting people and planet first, businesses can not only contribute to a better world but also gain a competitive advantage and secure their long-term viability.

The changing landscape of business in the 21st century demands a new approach. Purpose-driven businesses have emerged as leaders in this new era, driven by the rise of conscious consumerism, evolving stakeholder expectations, and the realization of economic and social benefits.

ϼϼϼ

"Success is no longer solely defined by financial gain, but by the positive impact we create in the world."

ϼϼϼ

Defining Your Purpose: Uncovering the Why

Understanding the importance of a clear and meaningful purpose
Identifying your company's values and mission
Aligning purpose with business strategy

❧❧❧

TWO

DEFINING YOUR PURPOSE: UNCOVERING THE WHY

Discovering and articulating your why—the reason your organization exists beyond making a profit—is crucial for becoming a purpose-driven business. Here I will explore the importance of a clear and meaningful purpose, how to identify your company's values and mission, and how to align purpose with your overall business strategy.

2.1 The Importance of a Clear and Meaningful Purpose:

A clear and meaningful purpose serves as the guiding star for your business. It goes beyond financial goals and encapsulates the positive impact you aim to create in the world. Your purpose should inspire and resonate with your stakeholders, including customers, employees, and investors. It provides a sense of direction, driving decision-making, strategy, and culture within your organization.

2.2 Identifying Your Company's Values and Mission:

Defining your purpose begins with understanding your company's values and mission. Values represent the core principles and beliefs that guide your organization's behavior. Mission outlines what your organization seeks to accomplish in pursuit of its purpose. By identifying and aligning these foundational elements, you create a solid framework for purpose-driven decision-making and action.

2.3 Uncovering the Why: Reflecting on Motivations and Impact:

Uncovering your why involves deep reflection on the motivations behind your business and the impact you aspire to make. Ask yourself and your team thought-provoking questions: What problem are you solving? How do you want to positively affect people's lives? What legacy do you want to leave behind? By exploring these questions, you can reveal the underlying purpose that drives your business.

2.4 Aligning Purpose with Business Strategy:

A purpose-driven business integrates its purpose into its overall business strategy. Purpose becomes a driving force behind product development, customer engagement, and operational decisions. By aligning purpose with strategy, you create coherence throughout your organization, ensuring that every aspect of your business serves your purpose and contributes to your desired impact.

2.5 Communicating Your Purpose Internally and Externally:

Once you have defined your purpose, it is crucial to communicate it effectively. Internally, your purpose should be shared with employees to create a sense of meaning and connection to their work. Externally, your purpose should be communicated to customers, investors, and other stakeholders to build trust and foster engagement. Authentic and compelling storytelling plays a vital role in communicating your purpose.

Defining your purpose is a pivotal step on the journey to becoming a purpose-driven business. It requires introspection, reflection, and alignment of your values and mission. A clear and meaningful purpose serves as a guiding light, driving your decisions, strategy, and culture. By communicating your purpose effectively, both internally and externally, you inspire and engage stakeholders who share your vision.

ᎶᎶᎶ

"A purpose-driven business is not just about making a profit, but about making a difference." - Richard Branson

ᎶᎶᎶ

Building a Purpose-Driven Culture: Engaging Your People

The role of leadership in fostering a purpose-driven culture
Employee engagement and empowerment
Nurturing a sense of community and shared values

❥❥❥

THREE

BUILDING A PURPOSE-DRIVEN CULTURE: ENGAGING YOUR PEOPLE

A purpose-driven culture fosters employee engagement, aligns values, and empowers individuals to contribute to the larger mission. We will discuss the role of leadership in shaping the culture, strategies for employee engagement and empowerment, and the importance of nurturing a sense of community and shared values.

3.1 The Role of Leadership in Fostering a Purpose-Driven Culture:

Leadership plays a vital role in shaping and nurturing a purpose-driven culture. Leaders must embody the organization's purpose, acting as role models and champions. They should communicate the purpose consistently, aligning it with the company's vision and values. By demonstrating authenticity and inspiring others, leaders create an environment where purpose thrives.

3.2 Employee Engagement and Empowerment:

Engaging employees in the purpose of the organization is key to building a purpose-driven culture. Employees should understand how their individual roles contribute to the larger mission and feel a sense of ownership and impact. This can be achieved through open communication, regular feedback, and opportunities for professional and personal growth. Empowering employees to make decisions and take initiative fosters a sense of purposeful autonomy.

3.3 Nurturing a Sense of Community and Shared Values:

Creating a strong sense of community and shared values is essential for a purpose-driven culture. Encouraging collaboration, teamwork, and a supportive work environment fosters a sense of belonging and collective purpose. Activities such as team-building exercises, volunteering initiatives, and shared celebrations help reinforce the shared values and sense of community within the organization.

3.4 Embedding Purpose in Daily Practices:

To truly embed purpose in the organizational culture, it must be integrated into daily practices and processes. This includes incorporating purpose into performance evaluations, setting goals and metrics aligned with the organization's mission, and recognizing and rewarding behaviors that exemplify the purpose. Purpose-driven organizations prioritize and actively promote ethical decision-making and responsible practices at all levels.

3.5 Overcoming Challenges and Sustaining a Purpose-Driven Culture:

Building and sustaining a purpose-driven culture is not without its challenges. It requires ongoing commitment, adaptation, and resilience. Leaders must address any barriers or resistance to change, communicate the benefits of a purpose-driven culture, and provide resources and support for employees to embrace and live the purpose. Regular evaluation and reinforcement of the culture are necessary to ensure its longevity.

Building a purpose-driven culture is instrumental in unleashing the full potential of your organization and its people. By fostering employee engagement and empowerment, aligning values, and nurturing a sense of community, you create an environment where purpose thrives. Effective leadership, daily practices that reflect purpose, and overcoming challenges contribute to a sustainable purpose-driven culture.

ꝒꝒꝒ

"Putting people and planet first is not a choice; it's an imperative for the future of business and society."

ꝒꝒꝒ

Creating Positive Impact: Sustainable Practices and Social Responsibility

Implementing environmentally sustainable initiatives
Social responsibility and ethical business practices
Collaboration and partnerships for greater impact

❧❧❧

FOUR

Creating Positive Impact: Sustainable Practices and Social Responsibility

As a purpose-driven business, it is crucial to align your operations with your purpose and contribute to a more sustainable and equitable world. We will explore the implementation of environmentally sustainable initiatives, the significance of social responsibility, and the power of collaboration and partnerships for greater impact.

4.1 Implementing Environmentally Sustainable Initiatives:

Environmental sustainability is a key aspect of creating positive impact. By implementing sustainable practices, businesses can reduce their carbon footprint, conserve resources, and minimize negative environmental impacts. This can include initiatives such as adopting renewable energy sources, reducing waste and promoting recycling, and optimizing supply chain processes to minimize ecological harm.

4.2 Social Responsibility and Ethical Business Practices:

Beyond environmental sustainability, social responsibility is another critical component of positive impact. Businesses must consider the social consequences of their actions and strive for ethical business practices. This involves fair treatment of employees, promoting diversity and inclusion, ensuring safe working conditions, and respecting human rights throughout the value chain. Social responsibility also extends to contributing to the well-being of local communities and addressing societal challenges.

4.3 Collaboration and Partnerships for Greater Impact:

Creating significant and lasting impact often requires collaboration and partnerships. By joining forces with like-minded organizations, businesses can amplify their positive influence. Collaborative initiatives can address complex social and environmental issues, leverage collective expertise and resources, and drive systemic change. Partnerships can range from local community organizations to cross-sector collaborations involving governments, nonprofits, and businesses.

4.4 Engaging Suppliers and Value Chain Responsibility:

A purpose-driven business takes responsibility for its entire value chain. Engaging suppliers and ensuring responsible practices throughout the supply chain is crucial for creating positive impact. This involves assessing and selecting suppliers based on their sustainability performance, working together to improve sustainability standards, and promoting transparency and accountability throughout the value chain.

4.5 Measuring and Reporting Impact:

To effectively create positive impact, it is essential to measure and report on your environmental and social performance. Implementing robust impact measurement systems allows businesses to track progress, identify areas for improvement, and communicate their achievements transparently. Reporting on environmental, social, and governance (ESG) performance provides stakeholders with valuable insights into the organization's commitment to positive impact.

Creating positive impact through sustainable practices and social responsibility is a core aspect of being a purpose-driven business. By implementing environmentally sustainable initiatives, prioritizing social responsibility, and fostering collaboration and partnerships, organizations can contribute to a more sustainable and equitable world. Engaging suppliers, measuring impact, and transparently reporting performance further demonstrate the commitment to positive change.

❧❧❧

"Purpose is the North Star that guides us, inspires us, and fuels our passion to make a difference." - Simon Sinek

❧❧❧

Innovating for a Better Future: Technology and Purpose

Harnessing technology to drive positive change
Innovations for sustainability and social impact
Balancing profit and purpose in the digital age

❧❧❧

FIVE

Innovating for a Better Future: Technology and Purpose

Technology has the potential to drive positive change and accelerate the impact of purpose-driven businesses. We will discuss harnessing technology for sustainability and social impact, innovations shaping the 21st century, and striking a balance between profit and purpose in the digital age.

5.1 Harnessing Technology to Drive Positive Change:

Technology offers unprecedented opportunities to address social and environmental challenges. Purpose-driven businesses can harness technology to develop innovative solutions that promote sustainability, social impact, and economic progress. Whether through advancements in renewable energy, smart cities, clean technologies, or digital platforms, technology can revolutionize industries and drive positive change at scale.

5.2 Innovations for Sustainability and Social Impact:

Innovation plays a crucial role in creating a better future. Purpose-driven businesses can leverage innovation to develop products, services, and business models that align with their purpose and address pressing societal and environmental needs. This can include eco-friendly products, circular economy initiatives, social enterprises, and technology-driven solutions that promote access to education, healthcare, and sustainable livelihoods.

5.3 Balancing Profit and Purpose in the Digital Age:

In the digital age, purpose-driven businesses face the challenge of balancing profit and purpose. Technology-driven platforms and business models have transformed industries and created immense wealth, but they can also raise ethical concerns and exacerbate inequality. Purpose-driven businesses must navigate this landscape by setting clear boundaries, ensuring transparency and accountability, and making conscious choices that align with their values and long-term impact.

5.4 Embracing Responsible and Ethical Technology Practices:

As technology continues to evolve, purpose-driven businesses must be mindful of responsible and ethical technology practices. This includes data privacy and security, fair and unbiased algorithms, and minimizing the negative social and environmental impacts of technological advancements. Purpose-driven organizations should actively engage in conversations and initiatives that shape the responsible use of technology for the benefit of all stakeholders.

5.5 Embracing Continuous Innovation and Adaptation:

Innovation is an ongoing process, and purpose-driven businesses must embrace continuous innovation and adaptation. They should foster a culture of learning, curiosity, and experimentation within their organizations. By staying ahead of technological advancements and societal shifts, purpose-driven businesses can remain relevant and continue making a positive impact in a rapidly changing world.

Technology presents immense opportunities for purpose-driven businesses to innovate and create a better future. By harnessing technology to drive positive change, developing innovations for sustainability and social impact, and balancing profit and purpose in the digital age, organizations can shape a more equitable and sustainable world. Embracing responsible technology practices and fostering a culture of continuous innovation are key to staying at the forefront of positive transformation.

ƤƤƤ

"A purpose-driven business is a force that transcends boundaries, unites people, and drives sustainable change."

ƤƤƤ

Stakeholder Engagement: Building Trust and Collaboration

Identifying and understanding your key stakeholders
Strategies for effective stakeholder engagement
Transparency, accountability, and trust-building

❥❥❥

SIX

STAKEHOLDER ENGAGEMENT: BUILDING TRUST AND COLLABORATION

Engaging effectively with stakeholders is crucial for building trust, fostering collaboration, and achieving long-term success. We will explore the identification and understanding of key stakeholders, strategies for effective stakeholder engagement, and the significance of transparency, accountability, and trust-building.

6.1 Identifying and Understanding Your Key Stakeholders:

Stakeholders are individuals or groups who have a vested interest in the success and impact of your business. Identifying and understanding your key stakeholders is a vital first step in effective engagement. Stakeholders can include customers, employees, investors, local communities, NGOs, government agencies, and more. By understanding their expectations, needs, and concerns, you can tailor your engagement strategies to create meaningful connections.

6.2 Strategies for Effective Stakeholder Engagement:

Engaging stakeholders effectively requires thoughtful planning and strategic approaches. It involves building relationships, listening actively, and involving stakeholders in decision-making processes. Some strategies for effective engagement include conducting stakeholder mapping exercises, holding regular dialogue sessions, establishing advisory boards or committees, and using various communication channels to facilitate open and transparent communication.

6.3 Transparency, Accountability, and Trust-Building:

Transparency and accountability are essential elements in stakeholder engagement. Purpose-driven businesses should strive for open and honest communication, sharing relevant information about their practices, impact, and decision-making processes. Being transparent builds trust with stakeholders and helps foster long-term relationships. Accountability involves delivering on commitments, addressing concerns, and taking responsibility for the social and environmental impact of your actions.

6.4 Collaborating for Greater Impact:

Collaboration with stakeholders is a powerful way to achieve greater impact. By partnering with stakeholders, purpose-driven businesses can leverage collective knowledge, resources, and expertise to address complex challenges. Collaborative initiatives can take the form of cross-sector partnerships, alliances with NGOs or government agencies, or engaging local communities in co-creation processes. Collaboration fosters shared ownership, enables broader perspectives, and generates innovative solutions.

6.5 Overcoming Challenges and Nurturing Long-Term Relationships:

Engaging stakeholders can present challenges such as conflicting interests, diverse perspectives, and evolving expectations. Purpose-driven businesses must proactively address these challenges, seeking common ground and building bridges for collaboration. Nurturing long-term relationships requires ongoing communication, demonstrating responsiveness to feedback, and continuously adapting engagement strategies to meet evolving stakeholder needs.

Effective stakeholder engagement is a cornerstone of building trust, fostering collaboration, and ensuring the long-term success of purpose-driven businesses. By identifying and understanding key stakeholders, implementing strategies for engagement, and emphasizing transparency, accountability, and trust-building, organizations can cultivate strong relationships with their stakeholders. Collaborating with stakeholders enables purpose-driven businesses to achieve greater impact and navigate complex challenges.

ᐅᐅᐅ

"When we put purpose at the center of our business, success becomes a byproduct of making a positive impact." - Arianna Huffington

ᐅᐅᐅ

The Business Case for Purpose: Financial and Competitive Advantages

Examining the financial benefits of purpose-driven business
Attracting and retaining talent
Gaining a competitive edge through purpose

ᗐᗐᗐ

SEVEN

The Business Case for Purpose: Financial and Competitive Advantages

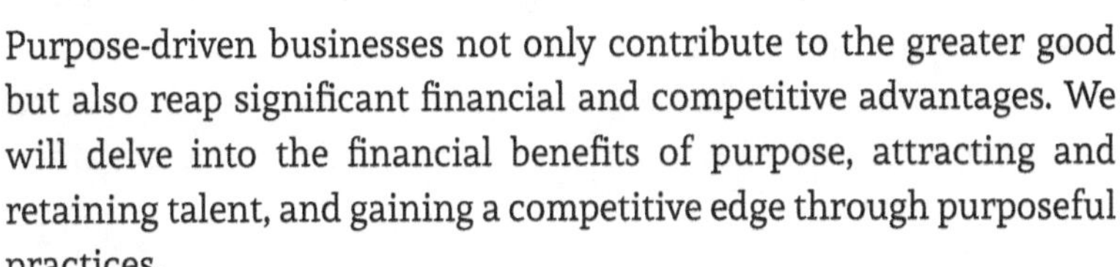

Purpose-driven businesses not only contribute to the greater good but also reap significant financial and competitive advantages. We will delve into the financial benefits of purpose, attracting and retaining talent, and gaining a competitive edge through purposeful practices.

7.1 The Financial Benefits of Purpose:

Contrary to the perception that purpose comes at the expense of financial success, purpose-driven businesses can achieve both positive societal impact and profitability. Research has shown that purpose-driven companies often outperform their peers in terms of financial performance, including revenue growth, return on investment, and stock market performance. Purpose attracts customers who align with the company's values, leading to increased loyalty and market share.

7.2 Attracting and Retaining Talent:

Purpose-driven businesses have a distinct advantage when it comes to attracting and retaining top talent. In the modern workforce, employees seek meaning and purpose in their work beyond financial compensation. Purpose-driven organizations that clearly articulate their mission and values appeal to individuals who are passionate about making a positive impact. This results in a higher level of employee engagement, satisfaction, and loyalty, leading to reduced turnover and increased productivity.

7.3 Gaining a Competitive Edge through Purpose:

Purpose-driven businesses differentiate themselves in a competitive marketplace. Consumers are increasingly making purchasing decisions based on values and are drawn to brands that demonstrate a genuine commitment to social and environmental impact. Purpose becomes a powerful differentiator that sets a business apart from its competitors. By integrating purpose into their brand identity, marketing strategies, and customer experience, purpose-driven businesses can attract and retain a loyal customer base.

7.4 Purpose as a Driver of Innovation and Adaptability:

Purpose drives innovation and fosters adaptability within an organization. When businesses have a clear purpose, they are motivated to continuously innovate and find creative solutions to address societal and environmental challenges. Purpose provides a guiding star for strategic decision-making, encouraging organizations to adapt to changing circumstances and seize emerging opportunities. This adaptability enhances a business's resilience and ability to thrive in a rapidly evolving business landscape.

7.5 Embracing Long-Term Sustainability:

Purpose-driven businesses prioritize long-term sustainability over short-term gains. By integrating purpose into their core strategies, organizations focus on building resilient business models that address environmental, social, and governance (ESG) considerations. This proactive approach to sustainability mitigates risks associated with environmental challenges, evolving consumer preferences, and regulatory changes. Purpose-driven businesses are better equipped to navigate disruptions and position themselves for long-term success.

The business case for purpose is compelling and multifaceted. Purpose-driven businesses not only make a positive societal impact but also enjoy financial benefits and gain a competitive edge. By attracting and retaining top talent, fostering innovation, and embracing long-term sustainability, purpose-driven organizations create a sustainable business model for the future.

ppp

"Purpose-driven businesses have the power to create a world where profit and purpose coexist harmoniously."

ppp

Communicating Your Purpose: Authenticity and Storytelling

Crafting a compelling purpose narrative
The power of authenticity in communication
Leveraging storytelling to engage stakeholders

❦❦❦

EIGHT

COMMUNICATING YOUR PURPOSE: AUTHENTICITY AND STORYTELLING

Communicating your purpose authentically and through compelling storytelling is essential for engaging stakeholders, building trust, and inspiring action. We will delve into the power of authenticity, crafting a purpose narrative, and leveraging storytelling to connect with your audience.

8.1 The Power of Authenticity in Communication:

Authenticity is the foundation of effective purpose-driven communication. Being authentic means aligning your words with your actions, demonstrating consistency, and staying true to your values. Authentic communication builds trust with stakeholders, as they can sense genuine intentions and a commitment to making a positive impact. Authenticity allows your purpose to resonate with your audience on a deeper level.

8.2 Crafting a Compelling Purpose Narrative:

A purpose narrative is the story that encapsulates your organization's purpose and impact. Crafting a compelling purpose narrative involves articulating your why, the journey that led you to your purpose, and the positive change you aspire to create. Your purpose narrative should be clear, concise, and emotionally resonant, allowing stakeholders to connect with your mission on a personal level.

8.3 Leveraging Storytelling to Engage Stakeholders:

Storytelling is a powerful tool for engaging stakeholders and bringing your purpose to life. Through stories, you can illustrate the impact of your work, evoke emotions, and create a sense of shared experience. Effective storytelling involves using narratives that highlight real-world examples, personal experiences, and compelling anecdotes. It enables stakeholders to connect with your purpose on an emotional level and motivates them to become advocates for your cause.

8.4 Communicating Across Different Channels and Platforms:

To effectively communicate your purpose, it is essential to leverage a variety of communication channels and platforms. This includes your website, social media, press releases, public speaking engagements, and internal communications. Tailor your messaging to each channel, ensuring consistency in tone and content while adapting to the unique characteristics of each platform. Consistent and multi-channel communication helps reach a broader audience and fosters engagement.

8.5 Engaging Employees as Purpose Ambassadors:

Employees play a crucial role in communicating your purpose.

Engaging and empowering them as purpose ambassadors strengthens your communication efforts. Provide employees with the knowledge, tools, and resources to articulate and live the purpose in their everyday work. Encourage them to share their own stories and experiences related to the purpose, further enhancing authenticity and building a strong purpose-driven culture.

Communicating your purpose authentically and through compelling storytelling is essential for connecting with stakeholders, building trust, and inspiring action. Authenticity establishes credibility and fosters trust, while storytelling brings your purpose to life and engages stakeholders on an emotional level. Leveraging various communication channels and engaging employees as purpose ambassadors amplifies your impact.

ᐒᐒᐒ

"Businesses that prioritize purpose attract employees, customers, and partners who believe in their mission and contribute to their success." - Tony Hsieh

ᐒᐒᐒ

Measuring Impact: Metrics and Reporting

Defining meaningful impact metrics
Reporting on environmental, social, and governance (ESG) performance
The evolving landscape of impact measurement

❧❧❧

NINE

MEASURING IMPACT: METRICS AND REPORTING

Measuring impact allows you to assess the effectiveness of your initiatives, make data-driven decisions, and communicate your progress transparently to stakeholders. We will discuss the definition of meaningful impact metrics, reporting on environmental, social, and governance (ESG) performance, and the evolving landscape of impact measurement.

9.1 Defining Meaningful Impact Metrics:

Meaningful impact metrics are key indicators that allow you to measure progress toward your purpose and assess the effectiveness of your initiatives. These metrics go beyond financial indicators and encompass social, environmental, and governance aspects. Examples of impact metrics can include carbon footprint reduction, employee satisfaction and well-being, diversity and inclusion metrics, community engagement, and supply chain sustainability performance. It is important to define metrics that align with your purpose and capture the outcomes that matter most to your stakeholders.

9.2 Reporting on Environmental, Social, and Governance (ESG) Performance:

Reporting on ESG performance has become essential for purpose-driven businesses. ESG reporting provides stakeholders with insights into the environmental, social, and governance practices of an organization. It demonstrates a commitment to responsible business conduct, transparency, and accountability. ESG reporting can include metrics related to energy consumption, waste management, employee diversity and inclusion, community investments, ethical sourcing, and governance structure. By reporting on ESG performance, businesses can showcase their efforts and progress in creating positive impact.

9.3 The Evolving Landscape of Impact Measurement:

The landscape of impact measurement is continuously evolving as businesses and stakeholders recognize the need for more robust assessment frameworks. Various methodologies and frameworks, such as the UN Sustainable Development Goals (SDGs), the Global Reporting Initiative (GRI), and the Impact Management Project (IMP), are emerging to guide organizations in measuring their impact effectively. It is important to stay informed about emerging standards and best practices to ensure your impact measurement aligns with industry expectations and remains relevant over time.

9.4 Integrating Impact Measurement into Decision-Making:

Measuring impact should not be a standalone process; it should be integrated into your organization's decision-making processes. By gathering and analyzing impact data, you gain valuable insights to inform strategic planning, resource allocation, and operational improvements. Impact measurement helps you understand which initiatives are most effective, identify areas for improvement, and make data-driven decisions that align with your purpose and drive greater impact.

9.5 Communicating Impact to Stakeholders:

Transparent and effective communication of impact is crucial for building trust and engaging stakeholders. Reporting on impact should go beyond sharing data; it should tell a compelling story about the positive change your business is making. Communicate your impact through various channels, such as annual reports, sustainability reports, dedicated impact reports, and digital platforms. Use clear and concise language, visualizations, and real-life examples to engage stakeholders and demonstrate the value of your purpose-driven efforts.

Measuring and reporting on the impact of your purpose-driven business is essential for assessing progress, making informed decisions, and building trust with stakeholders. Meaningful impact metrics go beyond financial indicators and encompass social, environmental, and governance aspects. Reporting on ESG performance demonstrates transparency and commitment to responsible business practices. As the landscape of impact measurement continues to evolve, it is important to stay updated on emerging frameworks and methodologies. Integrating impact measurement into decision-making and effectively communicating impact helps drive greater positive change.

ᐅᐅᐅ

"Being purpose-driven means being committed to creating a legacy that extends beyond our own lifetimes."

ᐅᐅᐅ

Investing in Purpose: Funding and Financing Models

Exploring purpose-driven investment opportunities
Socially responsible investing and impact funds
Strategies for securing funding for purpose-driven initiatives

❧❧❧

TEN

INVESTING IN PURPOSE: FUNDING AND FINANCING MODELS

Investing in purpose goes beyond traditional profit-driven approaches and seeks to align financial resources with social and environmental impact. We will discuss purpose-driven investment opportunities, socially responsible investing, impact funds, and strategies for securing funding for purpose-driven initiatives.

10.1 Exploring Purpose-Driven Investment Opportunities:

Purpose-driven businesses have access to a range of investment opportunities that prioritize both financial returns and positive impact. Impact investing involves allocating capital to businesses, organizations, and funds with the intention of generating measurable social or environmental impact alongside financial returns. Socially responsible investing focuses on investing in companies that align with specific environmental, social, and governance (ESG) criteria. By exploring purpose-driven investment opportunities, businesses can attract capital from investors who share their values and commitment to positive change.

10.2 Socially Responsible Investing and Impact Funds:

Socially responsible investing (SRI) and impact funds are key vehicles for funding purpose-driven initiatives. SRI involves investing in companies or funds that meet certain ESG criteria and demonstrate a commitment to sustainable practices. Impact funds are investment vehicles specifically designed to generate positive social and environmental impact alongside financial returns. These funds are managed by impact investors who seek measurable outcomes aligned with their investment thesis. Engaging with SRI and impact funds can provide access to capital and a network of investors who are specifically interested in supporting purpose-driven businesses.

10.3 Strategies for Securing Funding for Purpose-Driven Initiatives:

Securing funding for purpose-driven initiatives requires strategic planning and a comprehensive approach. Some strategies to consider include:

a) Building Relationships with Impact Investors: Establish connections with impact investors who are aligned with your purpose and mission. Attend impact-focused events, engage in impact investing networks, and leverage platforms that connect purpose-driven entrepreneurs with potential investors.

b) Leveraging Government Grants and Programs: Research and apply for government grants, subsidies, and programs that support businesses engaged in social and environmental impact. Many governments have specific funding initiatives for purpose-driven enterprises.

c) Crowdfunding and Community Engagement: Utilize crowdfunding platforms and engage your community to secure financial support. Crowdfunding allows individuals who resonate with your purpose to contribute to your initiatives, building a sense of ownership and support.

d) Partnerships and Collaborations: Forge partnerships with like-minded organizations, foundations, and impact-focused institutions. Collaborative efforts can not only share financial resources but also provide expertise, networks, and access to additional funding opportunities.

10.4 Balancing Financial Sustainability and Purpose:

Finding a balance between financial sustainability and purpose is essential for the long-term viability of purpose-driven businesses. While pursuing impact-driven initiatives, businesses need to ensure their revenue streams are sustainable and align with their purpose. It may involve exploring innovative business models, revenue diversification strategies, and seeking long-term partnerships with investors who understand and support the financial realities of purpose-driven enterprises.

10.5 Measurement and Reporting of Impact to Attract Funding:

Effectively measuring and reporting on the impact of your initiatives is critical in attracting funding for your purpose-driven business. Demonstrating the positive social and environmental outcomes of your work through robust impact measurement and transparent reporting enhances your credibility and increases investor confidence. Highlighting the financial and impact returns of your initiatives can attract investors who value both financial performance and purpose alignment.

Funding and financing models play a crucial role in supporting purpose-driven businesses. Exploring purpose-driven investment opportunities, engaging with socially responsible investing and impact funds, and implementing strategies for securing funding are essential steps for accessing capital aligned with your purpose. Balancing financial sustainability and purpose is crucial for long-term viability, and effective measurement and reporting of impact can attract investors who value positive social and environmental outcomes.

ppp

"When we align our business goals with a higher purpose, we unlock untapped potential for innovation, growth, and positive change." - John Mackey

ppp

Leading with Purpose: Inspiring Change from the Top

The role of purpose-driven leadership
Leading by example and fostering a purpose-driven mindset
Overcoming challenges and resistance to change

❧❧❧

ELEVEN

LEADING WITH PURPOSE: INSPIRING CHANGE FROM THE TOP

Effective leadership sets the tone, shapes the culture, and mobilizes the organization towards achieving its purpose. We will discuss the characteristics of purpose-driven leaders, strategies for leading with purpose, and the importance of leadership development in creating a purpose-driven organization.

11.1 Characteristics of Purpose-Driven Leaders:

Purpose-driven leaders possess specific qualities that enable them to inspire change and create a positive impact. They have a clear understanding of their own purpose and values, and they authentically align them with the purpose of the organization. These leaders demonstrate empathy, humility, and a genuine commitment to the well-being of their employees, stakeholders, and the wider community. They lead by example, embodying the purpose in their actions and decisions, and they have a vision that inspires and motivates others to contribute to a greater cause.

11.2 Strategies for Leading with Purpose:

Leading with purpose requires adopting specific strategies that drive meaningful change. Some strategies include:

a) Articulating and Communicating the Purpose:

Purpose-driven leaders effectively communicate the organization's purpose, ensuring clarity and understanding throughout the organization. They consistently convey the "why" behind the organization's work, inspiring a sense of shared purpose among employees and stakeholders.

b) Creating a Purpose-Driven Culture:

Purpose-driven leaders foster a culture that aligns with the organization's purpose. They create an environment where purpose is embedded in the organization's values, practices, and decision-making processes. This includes empowering employees, fostering collaboration, and recognizing and celebrating purpose-driven achievements.

c) Empowering and Engaging Employees:

Purpose-driven leaders empower and engage employees by providing them with autonomy, ownership, and opportunities to contribute to the purpose. They encourage and support professional growth and development, create avenues for employee input and feedback, and recognize and reward purpose-driven efforts.

d) Aligning Strategy with Purpose:

Purpose-driven leaders ensure that the organization's strategy is closely aligned with its purpose. They make strategic decisions that prioritize the organization's purpose, ensuring that all initiatives and actions contribute to the desired impact. Purpose-driven leaders also actively seek opportunities for innovation and adaptation to address evolving social and environmental challenges.

11.3 The Importance of Leadership Development:

Leadership development is crucial for creating a pipeline of purpose-driven leaders within the organization. Developing leaders who embrace purpose requires investing in their personal growth, skill development, and mindset transformation. This includes providing leadership training programs, mentoring, coaching, and opportunities for exposure to purpose-driven role models. Leadership development initiatives cultivate a strong leadership bench and ensure the continuity of purpose-driven leadership throughout the organization.

11.4 Overcoming Challenges and Leading Through Change:

Leading with purpose involves navigating challenges and leading through change effectively. Purpose-driven leaders must address resistance, manage competing priorities, and overcome obstacles to purposeful transformation. They remain resilient in the face of setbacks, adapt their strategies as needed, and inspire and empower their teams to embrace change and stay committed to the purpose.

11.5 Inspiring a Movement: Leading Beyond the Organization:

Purpose-driven leaders have the potential to inspire a movement that extends beyond their organization. They can become advocates for purpose in the wider business community and society. By sharing their experiences, insights, and successes, purpose-driven leaders influence and inspire others to adopt purpose-driven practices and create positive impact. They collaborate with like-minded leaders, engage in industry discussions, and participate in initiatives that drive purposeful change on a larger scale.

Leading with purpose is a transformative force that drives the success and impact of purpose-driven businesses. Purpose-driven leaders embody the organization's purpose, inspire change, and create a positive culture. By articulating the purpose, fostering a purpose-driven culture, empowering employees, aligning strategy with purpose, and investing in leadership development, purpose-driven leaders can drive meaningful change within their organizations and inspire a wider movement.

ᐅᐅᐅ

"Purpose-driven businesses understand that success is not measured solely by shareholder value, but by the value we bring to society."

ᐅᐅᐅ

Purposeful Marketing: Building Brands that Matter

The role of purpose in brand differentiation
Marketing strategies for purpose-driven businesses
Engaging customers through purposeful storytelling

❥❥❥

TWELVE

PURPOSEFUL MARKETING: BUILDING BRANDS THAT MATTER

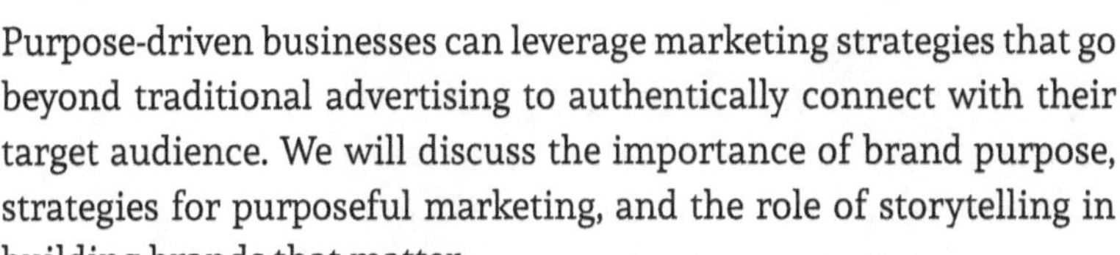

Purpose-driven businesses can leverage marketing strategies that go beyond traditional advertising to authentically connect with their target audience. We will discuss the importance of brand purpose, strategies for purposeful marketing, and the role of storytelling in building brands that matter.

12.1 The Importance of Brand Purpose:

Brand purpose is the underlying reason why a business exists beyond making a profit. It represents the positive impact a brand aims to create in the world. A clear and meaningful brand purpose sets the foundation for purposeful marketing. It helps differentiate the brand, attracts like-minded customers, and fosters loyalty. Brand purpose guides marketing efforts, ensuring that all messaging and initiatives align with the core values and mission of the organization.

12.2 Strategies for Purposeful Marketing:

Purposeful marketing involves strategies that authentically connect with consumers, communicate the brand purpose, and inspire action. Some strategies to consider include:

a) Authentic Storytelling:

Tell compelling stories that showcase the brand's purpose and impact. Use storytelling to create an emotional connection with your audience, highlighting real-life examples, personal narratives, and the positive change your brand is making. Authentic storytelling evokes empathy, inspires action, and fosters a deeper connection with your target audience.

b) Engaging Stakeholders:

Purposeful marketing involves engaging stakeholders in meaningful ways. Involve your customers, employees, and community in co-creation processes, feedback opportunities, and advocacy initiatives. Encourage user-generated content, testimonials, and social media conversations that amplify the brand purpose and create a sense of community around it.

c) Social and Environmental Activism:

Purposeful marketing can involve taking a stance on social and environmental issues that align with the brand purpose. By actively supporting causes, advocating for positive change, and engaging in sustainability initiatives, brands can position themselves as agents of progress and attract consumers who value social and environmental responsibility.

d) Collaborative Partnerships:

Collaborate with like-minded organizations, nonprofits, or social enterprises to amplify the brand purpose and extend its impact. Strategic partnerships can create shared value, expand the reach of purposeful initiatives, and demonstrate the brand's commitment to collaboration and collective action.

12.3 Building Trust and Authenticity:

Trust and authenticity are paramount in purposeful marketing. Consumers today value transparency and expect brands to be genuine in their intentions and actions. Building trust involves consistently delivering on brand promises, being transparent about the brand's impact and practices, and actively listening to and addressing consumer feedback. Authenticity is crucial in every aspect of marketing, from messaging and visual identity to partnerships and community engagement.

12.4 Leveraging Digital Platforms:

Digital platforms provide immense opportunities for purposeful marketing. Social media, websites, and online communities allow brands to share their purpose-driven stories, engage with customers in real-time, and amplify their impact. Leveraging digital platforms also enables brands to target specific audiences, measure the effectiveness of marketing efforts, and foster two-way communication with stakeholders.

12.5 Measuring and Communicating Impact:

Measuring and communicating the impact of purposeful marketing efforts is essential for building credibility and engaging stakeholders. Develop metrics to assess the effectiveness of purposeful marketing initiatives, such as brand sentiment, customer engagement, and social media interactions. Communicate impact through transparent reporting, storytelling, and visual representations that highlight the positive change your brand is making.

Purposeful marketing is a powerful tool for building brands that matter. By aligning marketing strategies with brand purpose, authentically engaging stakeholders, and leveraging storytelling, purpose-driven businesses can connect with their target audience on a deeper level. Building trust and authenticity, leveraging digital platforms, and measuring and communicating impact contribute to the success of purposeful marketing efforts.

ᗡᗡᗡ

"Purpose is the fuel that ignites passion, resilience, and unwavering determination in the pursuit of making a difference."

ᗡᗡᗡ

Collaboration for Greater Impact: Partnerships and Alliances

The power of collaboration in achieving purpose-driven goals
Forging strategic partnerships with like-minded organizations
Collective action for systemic change

❧❧❧

THIRTEEN

COLLABORATION FOR GREATER IMPACT: PARTNERSHIPS AND ALLIANCES

By forming partnerships and alliances, organizations can leverage collective resources, expertise, and networks to tackle complex social and environmental challenges. We will discuss the benefits of collaboration, strategies for successful partnerships, and the role of alliances in amplifying impact.

13.1 The Benefits of Collaboration:

Collaboration brings numerous benefits to purpose-driven businesses. Some key benefits include:

a) Leveraging Collective Resources:

Collaboration allows organizations to pool together their resources, whether it's financial, human, or intellectual capital. By combining forces, partners can achieve greater efficiency, scale their impact, and tackle larger-scale projects that would be challenging to accomplish alone.

b) Sharing Expertise and Knowledge:

Collaborating with diverse partners brings together different perspectives, expertise, and knowledge. This diversity of ideas can lead to innovative solutions, fresh insights, and increased learning opportunities. Collaborative efforts enable organizations to tap into the strengths and specialized skills of their partners, fostering continuous improvement and growth.

c) Amplifying Reach and Influence:

Partnerships and alliances provide access to broader networks and audiences. By joining forces with organizations that have complementary missions and target audiences, businesses can expand their reach and influence, generating more awareness and support for their purpose-driven initiatives. Collaborative efforts often attract more attention and generate greater impact than individual endeavors.

d) Enhancing Credibility and Trust:

Collaboration with reputable and like-minded organizations enhances credibility and builds trust among stakeholders. Being part of a collaborative effort demonstrates a commitment to collective action and a shared purpose. This can strengthen relationships with customers, employees, investors, and the wider community, increasing confidence in the organization's ability to create meaningful change.

13.2 Strategies for Successful Partnerships:

Forming successful partnerships requires careful planning and nurturing. Consider the following strategies:

a) Shared Vision and Values:

Ensure that potential partners share a common vision and values alignment. Clarify each organization's purpose and identify areas of mutual interest and synergy. A shared understanding of goals and values forms the foundation for a strong partnership.

b) Clear Objectives and Roles:

Establish clear objectives and define the roles and responsibilities of each partner. Clearly articulate what each partner brings to the table, leveraging their unique strengths and expertise. This clarity helps avoid misunderstandings and ensures a harmonious collaboration.

c) Open Communication and Trust:

Foster open and transparent communication among partners. Establish channels for regular communication, feedback, and decision-making. Build trust by honoring commitments, being responsive, and maintaining open lines of dialogue.

d) Mutual Benefit and Win-Win Solutions:

Strive for mutually beneficial outcomes and win-win solutions. Collaboration should result in shared value creation, with each partner gaining something of value from the partnership. Seek opportunities to leverage shared resources, expertise, and networks for maximum impact.

13.3 The Role of Alliances in Amplifying Impact:

Alliances play a crucial role in amplifying the impact of purpose-driven businesses. Alliances are formed by organizations with similar missions or interests, coming together to achieve common objectives. These collective efforts can address systemic challenges, advocate for policy changes, and create industry-wide impact. Alliances provide a platform for sharing knowledge, coordinating efforts, and influencing stakeholders at a larger scale.

13.4 Overcoming Challenges in Collaboration:

Collaboration can present challenges such as conflicting priorities, differing organizational cultures, and potential power dynamics. To overcome these challenges, it is important to foster a spirit of collaboration, establish clear communication channels, and proactively address any issues that arise. Building trust, practicing active listening, and maintaining a shared focus on the collective impact can help navigate and resolve challenges in collaborative partnerships.

13.5 Long-Term Sustainability of Collaborative Efforts:

Sustaining collaborative efforts requires ongoing commitment and nurturing. Regularly evaluate the impact and effectiveness of the partnership, and adjust strategies as needed. Foster a culture of collaboration within the organization and seek opportunities to engage new partners or expand existing alliances. Long-term sustainability of collaborative efforts is achieved by continuously learning, adapting, and reinforcing the shared vision and purpose.

Collaboration through partnerships and alliances has the power to drive greater impact for purpose-driven businesses. By leveraging collective resources, sharing expertise, amplifying reach, and enhancing credibility, collaboration enhances the effectiveness and scale of purpose-driven initiatives. Successful partnerships require shared vision, clear objectives, open communication, and mutual benefit. Alliances further amplify impact by mobilizing collective efforts and influencing stakeholders on a larger scale. Overcoming challenges and ensuring the long-term sustainability of collaborative efforts contribute to creating lasting change.

ᐅᐅᐅ

"Purpose-driven leaders inspire others to join their cause, creating a ripple effect that amplifies impact and transforms communities."

ᐅᐅᐅ

Purposeful Innovation: Designing Products and Services for Good

Integrating purpose into product and service development
Design thinking for social and environmental impact
The potential of circular economy and sustainable business models

❧❧❧

FOURTEEN

Purposeful Innovation: Designing Products and Services for Good

Purpose-driven businesses leverage innovation to create solutions that address pressing challenges while aligning with their core values. We will discuss the principles of purposeful innovation, strategies for integrating purpose into the design process, and the importance of user-centricity in creating products and services for good.

14.1 The Principles of Purposeful Innovation:

Purposeful innovation is driven by the intention to create products and services that generate positive impact. The principles of purposeful innovation include:

a) Human-Centered Design:

Prioritize the needs, values, and aspirations of users throughout the design process. Understand their pain points, desires, and behaviors to create solutions that truly meet their needs.

b) Sustainable Practices:

Integrate sustainability principles into the design and development of products and services. Consider the lifecycle impact, materials sourcing, energy efficiency, and end-of-life disposal to minimize negative environmental consequences.

c) Social Impact Orientation:

Identify social issues that align with the organization's purpose and leverage innovation to address them. Design products and services that contribute to positive social change, such as improving access to education, healthcare, or clean energy.

d) Ethical Considerations:

Embed ethical considerations into the design process, ensuring products and services uphold principles of fairness, inclusivity, and responsible use of technology. Consider potential unintended consequences and strive to minimize negative impacts on individuals and communities.

14.2 Integrating Purpose into the Design Process:

Integrating purpose into the design process requires a deliberate and holistic approach. Some strategies to consider include:

a) Defining Purposeful Design Objectives:

Clearly articulate the purpose-driven objectives for the product or service. Establish the intended impact, target audience, and desired outcomes. This provides a guiding framework for the design process.

b) Conducting User Research and Co-creation:

Engage with users and stakeholders to understand their needs, preferences, and aspirations. Involve them in the design process through co-creation workshops, feedback sessions, and iterative prototyping. Incorporate their insights to ensure user-centricity and relevance.

c) Applying Sustainable Design Principles:

Integrate sustainable design principles into the product development process. Consider factors such as materials selection, energy efficiency, waste reduction, and recyclability. Strive for circular economy models that promote resource efficiency and minimize environmental impact.

d) Embracing Technological Innovations:

Embrace technological advancements that can enhance the purpose and impact of products and services. Leverage emerging technologies like artificial intelligence, blockchain, or renewable energy to create innovative solutions that address social and environmental challenges.

14.3 User-Centricity and Co-design:

User-centricity is essential in purposeful innovation. By deeply understanding the needs, values, and aspirations of users, businesses can design products and services that truly resonate. Co-design, involving users as active participants in the design process, ensures that the end result meets their specific requirements and preferences. User feedback and usability testing provide valuable insights for iterative improvement and refinement.

14.4 Measuring and Evaluating Impact:

Measuring and evaluating the impact of purposeful innovation is crucial for understanding the effectiveness and value of products and services. Develop metrics and evaluation frameworks that capture the intended social and environmental outcomes. Consider indicators such as improved quality of life, reduced environmental footprint, increased access to resources, or behavior change. Regularly assess and report on the impact to drive continuous improvement and transparency.

14.5 Scaling Purposeful Innovation:

Scaling purposeful innovation requires a strategic approach. Consider the following strategies:

a) Strategic Partnerships:

Collaborate with like-minded organizations, research institutions, or government agencies to scale the impact of purposeful innovation. Leverage their resources, expertise, and networks to reach larger audiences and expand the adoption of innovative solutions.

b) Open Innovation and Co-creation Platforms:

Open up the innovation process by engaging external stakeholders through co-creation platforms, hackathons, or open innovation challenges. Tap into the collective intelligence and creativity of a broader community to generate novel ideas and accelerate innovation.

c) Accessibility and Affordability:

Ensure that purposeful products and services are accessible and affordable to a wide range of users. Consider inclusive pricing models, partnerships with NGOs or government programs, or design approaches that prioritize affordability without compromising quality or impact.

Purposeful innovation allows businesses to design products and services that create positive social and environmental impact. By embracing principles of human-centered design, sustainability, social impact, and ethical considerations, purpose-driven businesses can drive innovation that addresses pressing challenges. Integrating purpose into the design process, prioritizing user-centricity, and measuring impact contribute to the success of purposeful innovation. Scaling purposeful innovation involves strategic partnerships, open innovation approaches, and ensuring accessibility and affordability.

ppp

"Businesses that put people and the planet first create a virtuous cycle of prosperity that benefits all stakeholders." - Patagonia

ppp

Ethical Leadership: Navigating Moral Dilemmas and Tough Choices

Ethical decision-making in purpose-driven businesses
Balancing stakeholder interests and ethical considerations
Case studies in ethical leadership

ᐅᐅᐅ

FIFTEEN

Ethical Leadership: Navigating Moral Dilemmas and Tough Choices

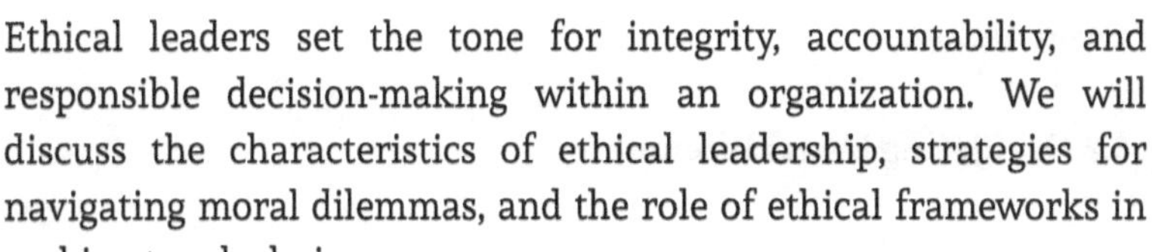

Ethical leaders set the tone for integrity, accountability, and responsible decision-making within an organization. We will discuss the characteristics of ethical leadership, strategies for navigating moral dilemmas, and the role of ethical frameworks in making tough choices.

15.1 Characteristics of Ethical Leadership:

Ethical leaders demonstrate certain key characteristics that guide their decision-making and actions. These include:

a) Integrity and Transparency:

Ethical leaders act with honesty, consistency, and transparency in all their interactions. They adhere to high moral and ethical principles, setting an example for others to follow.

b) Accountability and Responsibility:

Ethical leaders take ownership of their decisions and actions. They accept responsibility for the consequences of their choices and are willing to be held accountable for their behavior.

c) Empathy and Respect:

Ethical leaders demonstrate empathy and respect for others. They consider the impact of their decisions on stakeholders and actively listen to diverse perspectives before making judgments.

d) Fairness and Justice:

Ethical leaders promote fairness and justice in their decision-making processes. They treat individuals equitably, without favoritism or bias, and ensure that all stakeholders are given equal consideration.

15.2 Navigating Moral Dilemmas:

Moral dilemmas are situations where leaders are faced with conflicting ethical considerations or choices. Ethical leaders navigate these dilemmas by employing the following strategies:

a) Ethical Reflection:

Engage in deep introspection and ethical reflection when faced with a moral dilemma. Consider the underlying values, principles, and potential consequences of each available choice.

b) Seek Diverse Perspectives:

Gather input and insights from diverse stakeholders who may be impacted by the decision. Encourage open dialogue, actively listen to different viewpoints, and consider the ethical implications from multiple angles.

c) Ethical Frameworks:

Utilize ethical frameworks or decision-making models to guide the evaluation of moral dilemmas. Examples of frameworks include utilitarianism, deontology, and virtue ethics. These frameworks provide a structured approach to analyzing ethical choices and their potential impact.

d) Consult with Ethics Experts:

Seek guidance from ethics experts or engage an ethics committee within the organization. These individuals can provide informed perspectives, ethical analysis, and assist in evaluating potential consequences and risks.

15.3 Making Tough Choices:

Ethical leaders often face tough choices that require balancing competing values or priorities. Strategies for making tough choices include:

a) Prioritize Core Values:

Identify the core values and principles that guide the organization's purpose. Use these values as a foundation for decision-making and prioritize them when faced with conflicting options.

b) Long-Term Impact Assessment:

Consider the long-term impact of each choice, both in terms of ethical considerations and the organization's overall purpose. Evaluate potential consequences, risks, and benefits to make choices that align with long-term sustainability and positive impact.

c) Stakeholder Engagement:

Engage with key stakeholders to understand their perspectives, concerns, and aspirations. Consider their input when making tough choices, ensuring that decisions are responsive to their needs and values.

d) Ethical Courage:

Demonstrate ethical courage in making tough choices. Ethical leaders are willing to make difficult decisions even when they may face opposition or short-term challenges. They prioritize integrity and the long-term well-being of the organization and its stakeholders over personal or immediate gain.

15.4 Fostering an Ethical Culture:

Ethical leaders play a vital role in fostering an ethical culture within the organization. Strategies for fostering an ethical culture include:

a) Lead by Example:

Ethical leaders embody the values and behaviors they expect from others. They consistently demonstrate ethical conduct and integrity in their actions, serving as role models for ethical behavior.

b) Establish Clear Ethical Guidelines:

Develop and communicate clear ethical guidelines and standards within the organization. These guidelines should articulate the expected ethical behavior, outline procedures for reporting ethical concerns, and provide guidance for decision-making.

c) Ethical Training and Education:

Provide ongoing ethical training and education to employees. Offer opportunities for discussion and learning on ethical dilemmas, case studies, and ethical decision-making processes. This helps build ethical awareness and equips employees with the skills to navigate moral challenges.

d) Reward Ethical Behavior:

Recognize and reward ethical behavior and integrity within the organization. This reinforces the importance of ethical conduct and encourages employees to uphold ethical standards.

15.5 Learning and Adaptation:

Ethical leaders embrace continuous learning and adaptation. They actively seek feedback, evaluate the consequences of their choices, and adjust their approach when needed. Ethical leaders remain open to new perspectives, reflect on their own biases, and strive to improve their ethical decision-making skills over time.

Ethical leadership is crucial in guiding purpose-driven businesses through moral dilemmas and tough choices. Ethical leaders embody characteristics such as integrity, transparency, empathy, and fairness. They navigate moral dilemmas by engaging in ethical reflection, seeking diverse perspectives, and utilizing ethical frameworks. When faced with tough choices, ethical leaders prioritize core values, assess long-term impact, engage stakeholders, and demonstrate ethical courage. Fostering an ethical culture is essential, and ethical leaders play a key role in leading by example, establishing clear guidelines, providing ethical training, and rewarding ethical behavior. Continuous learning and adaptation are fundamental for ethical leadership.

 PPP

"Purpose-driven businesses have the power to drive societal change and shape a future that is sustainable, equitable, and compassionate."

PPP

Engaging the Local Community: Impact at a Grassroots Level

Building strong relationships with local communities
Investing in community development and well-being
Empowering and supporting local initiatives

❦❦❦

SIXTEEN

ENGAGING THE LOCAL COMMUNITY: IMPACT AT A GRASSROOTS LEVEL

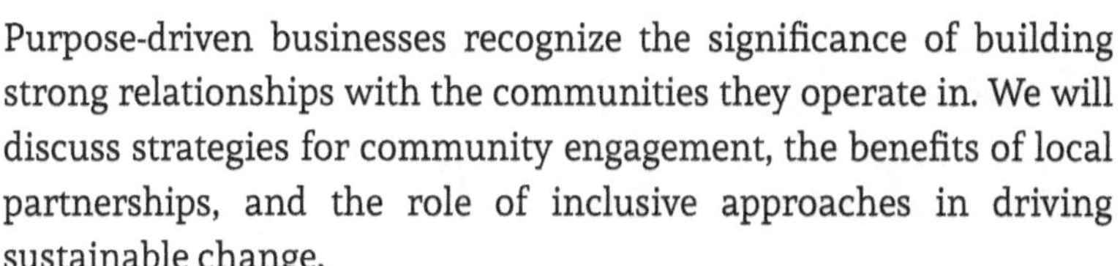

Purpose-driven businesses recognize the significance of building strong relationships with the communities they operate in. We will discuss strategies for community engagement, the benefits of local partnerships, and the role of inclusive approaches in driving sustainable change.

16.1 Understanding the Local Community:

To engage the local community effectively, purpose-driven businesses must first understand the unique characteristics, needs, and aspirations of the community they are operating in. Conducting thorough research, engaging in dialogue, and actively listening to community members helps establish a solid foundation for meaningful engagement.

16.2 Strategies for Community Engagement:

Effective community engagement requires intentional strategies that foster trust, collaboration, and shared decision-making. Some strategies to consider include:

a) Building Relationships:

Take the time to build relationships with community members, local organizations, and leaders. Engage in open dialogue, attend community events, and participate in local initiatives. Building trust and understanding is essential for successful community engagement.

b) Co-creation and Participation:

Involve community members in decision-making processes and project planning through co-creation and participatory approaches. Seek input, feedback, and ideas from the community to ensure that initiatives align with their needs and aspirations.

c) Education and Empowerment:

Offer educational programs, skill-building workshops, and resources that empower community members. By providing opportunities for personal and professional development, businesses can contribute to the growth and well-being of the local community.

d) Social Impact Initiatives:

Design and implement social impact initiatives that address specific challenges identified within the community. Collaborate with local organizations, nonprofits, and community leaders to develop programs that create positive change and generate a sense of ownership and pride among community members.

16.3 Benefits of Local Partnerships:

Local partnerships play a vital role in community engagement and impact at a grassroots level. Collaborating with local organizations and stakeholders brings several benefits, including:

a) Local Knowledge and Expertise:

Local partners possess valuable knowledge about the community, its culture, and its unique challenges. Their expertise can inform the design and implementation of initiatives, ensuring they are contextually relevant and effective.

b) Shared Resources and Networks:

Local partnerships provide access to shared resources, networks, and capabilities. By combining forces, businesses and local partners can amplify their impact, reach a wider audience, and leverage each other's strengths.

c) Credibility and Trust:

Partnering with local organizations and community leaders enhances credibility and builds trust among community members. Local partners can vouch for the authenticity and sincerity of purpose-driven businesses, facilitating deeper community engagement and acceptance.

d) Sustainability and Long-Term Impact:

Local partnerships promote sustainability and long-term impact. By collaborating with local stakeholders, businesses can create initiatives that are designed to address long-standing community needs and contribute to the overall well-being of the community.

16.4 Inclusive Approaches for Sustainable Change:

Inclusive approaches are crucial for driving sustainable change at the grassroots level. Businesses should strive to ensure that their community engagement efforts are inclusive and respectful of diverse perspectives, needs, and voices. Consider the following approaches:

a) Cultural Sensitivity:

Respect and value the local culture, traditions, and customs. Adapt initiatives and communication to align with cultural norms, ensuring that they are inclusive and sensitive to the local context.

b) Diversity and Inclusion:

Embrace diversity and actively include marginalized groups within the community. Create opportunities for underrepresented individuals to participate, contribute, and benefit from purpose-driven initiatives.

c) Collaboration with Community Leaders:

Engage with community leaders who have a deep understanding of the local context and possess the trust and respect of community members. Collaborating with community leaders ensures that initiatives are aligned with community aspirations and have a greater chance of success.

d) Listening and Feedback Mechanisms:

Establish mechanisms for ongoing feedback and dialogue with the community. Actively listen to community members' concerns, suggestions, and needs, and integrate their input into decision-making processes. This fosters a sense of ownership and empowerment within the community.

16.5 Measuring and Communicating Community Impact:

Measuring and communicating the impact of community engagement efforts is essential for transparency and accountability. Develop metrics and indicators that capture the social, economic, and environmental outcomes of purpose-driven initiatives. Regularly evaluate and report on the progress and impact, sharing the results with the community and relevant stakeholders. Effective communication ensures that community members understand the value and positive change created through their collaboration.

Engaging the local community is crucial for purpose-driven businesses to create meaningful impact at a grassroots level. Understanding the local community, employing effective community engagement strategies, and fostering local partnerships are key steps in driving sustainable change. Inclusive approaches that respect local culture, embrace diversity, and collaborate with community leaders promote the long-term success and acceptance of purpose-driven initiatives. Measuring and communicating community impact ensures transparency and accountability.

ᗡᗡᗡ

"When we align our personal values with our work, every day becomes an opportunity to make a meaningful difference."

❦❦❦

The Future of Purpose: Trends and Predictions

Emerging trends in purpose-driven business
The potential impact of technology and globalization
Predictions for the future of purpose-driven business

ᐅᐅᐅ

SEVENTEEN

THE FUTURE OF PURPOSE: TRENDS AND PREDICTIONS

As the world continues to evolve, purpose-driven businesses are expected to play an increasingly significant role in driving positive change. We will discuss key trends such as conscious consumerism, technology advancements, sustainable practices, and the integration of purpose across industries.

17.1 Conscious Consumerism:

Conscious consumerism is a growing trend where consumers prioritize values and purpose when making purchasing decisions. In the future, this trend is expected to continue gaining momentum, influencing consumer expectations and shaping market dynamics. Consumers will increasingly seek out purpose-driven brands that align with their values, demonstrating social and environmental responsibility. Purpose-driven businesses that authentically communicate their mission and engage with consumers on a deeper level will thrive in this evolving landscape.

17.2 Technology Advancements:

Advancements in technology are poised to significantly impact the future of purpose-driven business. Technological innovations such as artificial intelligence, blockchain, and data analytics offer new opportunities for organizations to drive positive change. These technologies can enable greater transparency, efficiency, and impact measurement, allowing purpose-driven businesses to make informed decisions and demonstrate their social and environmental outcomes. Additionally, technology can facilitate communication, collaboration, and knowledge-sharing among stakeholders, amplifying the collective efforts towards achieving shared goals.

17.3 Sustainable Practices and Circular Economy:

The focus on sustainability and the circular economy will continue to shape the future of purpose-driven business. Organizations will increasingly adopt sustainable practices throughout their value chains, from sourcing materials to production, distribution, and end-of-life disposal. Embracing circular economy principles, such as reducing waste, reusing materials, and promoting product longevity, will become standard practice. Purpose-driven businesses will prioritize resource efficiency, renewable energy, and responsible consumption to mitigate their environmental impact and contribute to a more sustainable future.

17.4 Integration of Purpose Across Industries:

The integration of purpose across industries will become more prevalent in the future. Purpose-driven approaches will extend beyond traditional sectors such as social enterprises and nonprofits, and will permeate various industries. Companies across sectors will recognize the importance of integrating purpose into their business models, strategies, and operations. Purpose-driven initiatives, such as impact investing, sustainable supply chains, and corporate social responsibility, will become standard practices across diverse industries, driving positive change on a broader scale.

17.5 Collaboration and Cross-Sector Partnerships:

Collaboration and cross-sector partnerships will play a pivotal role in the future of purpose-driven business. Recognizing the interconnected nature of social and environmental challenges, organizations will increasingly collaborate with stakeholders from various sectors, including governments, nonprofits, academia, and community organizations. These collaborations will leverage diverse expertise, resources, and networks to address complex issues collectively. Purpose-driven businesses will actively seek out partnerships that amplify their impact, foster innovation, and drive systemic change.

17.6 Shift in Organizational Culture and Leadership:

The future of purpose-driven business will witness a shift in organizational culture and leadership. Businesses will prioritize purpose and values, embedding them into their organizational DNA. Ethical leadership, transparency, and stakeholder engagement will be key drivers of success. Purpose-driven businesses will cultivate a culture of collaboration, diversity, and inclusion, fostering an environment where employees are empowered to contribute to meaningful impact. Purposeful leadership will inspire and guide organizations through change, navigating ethical dilemmas and driving the integration of purpose into all aspects of business operations.

17.7 Evolving Metrics and Impact Measurement:

Metrics and impact measurement will continue to evolve in the future, allowing purpose-driven businesses to effectively communicate their impact. Traditional financial metrics will be complemented by robust frameworks that capture social and environmental outcomes. Organizations will strive for standardized impact measurement methodologies, enabling comparisons and benchmarking across industries. With advancements in technology, real-time impact reporting will become more prevalent, providing stakeholders with transparent and up-to-date information on the social and environmental performance of purpose-driven businesses.

The future of purpose-driven business is exciting and filled with potential. As conscious consumerism, technology advancements, sustainable practices, and cross-sector collaborations continue to shape the landscape, purpose-driven businesses will have opportunities to make a significant impact. By embracing these trends, fostering purpose-driven cultures, and adapting to evolving metrics and impact measurement, businesses can thrive in a future where purpose and positive change are at the core."Purpose is not just a mission statement; it is the driving force behind every decision and action we take in our business."

ᕗᕗᕗ

"Purpose is not just a mission statement; it is the driving force behind every decision and action we take in our business."

ᕗᕗᕗ

Overcoming Challenges: Lessons from Purpose-Driven Entrepreneurs

Real-life stories of purpose-driven entrepreneurs
Common challenges and how to overcome them
Lessons and insights for aspiring purpose-driven leaders

ᐅᐅᐅ

EIGHTEEN

OVERCOMING CHALLENGES: LESSONS FROM PURPOSE-DRIVEN ENTREPRENEURS

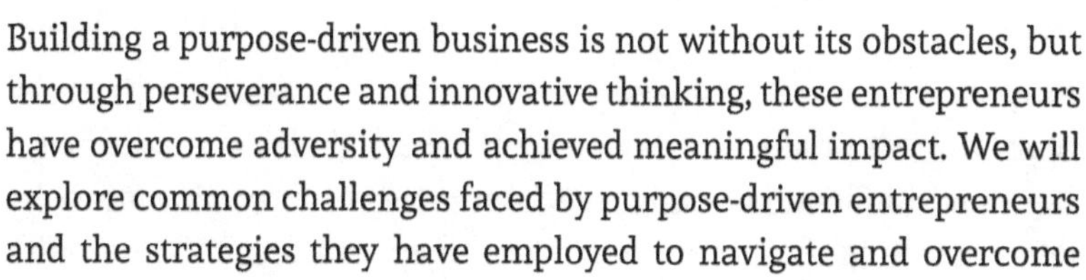

Building a purpose-driven business is not without its obstacles, but through perseverance and innovative thinking, these entrepreneurs have overcome adversity and achieved meaningful impact. We will explore common challenges faced by purpose-driven entrepreneurs and the strategies they have employed to navigate and overcome them.

18.1 Navigating Funding and Financial Challenges:

One common challenge for purpose-driven entrepreneurs is securing funding and managing financial resources. Purpose-driven ventures often face unique financing requirements and may encounter difficulty in accessing traditional funding sources. However, purpose-driven entrepreneurs have discovered strategies to overcome these challenges:

a) Alternative Funding Models:

Purpose-driven entrepreneurs have explored alternative funding models such as impact investing, crowdfunding, social impact bonds, and grants from foundations or impact-focused organizations. These models align with their values and attract investors who prioritize social and environmental impact alongside financial returns.

b) Revenue Generation Strategies:

Purpose-driven entrepreneurs focus on developing sustainable revenue models that align with their mission. They innovate and explore diverse income streams, such as fee-for-service models, partnerships, or product sales, to generate financial resources that support their social and environmental objectives.

c) Financial Management:

Purpose-driven entrepreneurs prioritize effective financial management practices. They develop financial plans, monitor cash flow, and implement strategies to optimize resource allocation. By demonstrating fiscal responsibility, they build credibility with stakeholders and attract support from investors and partners.

18.2 Scaling Impact and Growth: Scaling impact is a significant challenge for purpose-driven entrepreneurs, as they seek to expand their reach and create sustainable change. Purpose-driven entrepreneurs have adopted strategies to overcome the scaling challenge:

a) Collaborative Partnerships:

Purpose-driven entrepreneurs recognize the power of collaboration and strategic partnerships. By joining forces with like-minded organizations, they leverage complementary resources, expertise, and networks to scale their impact. Collaborative partnerships amplify their reach, enhance operational efficiency, and enable collective problem-solving.

b) Innovation and Technology:

Purpose-driven entrepreneurs harness the potential of innovation and technology to scale their impact. They leverage digital platforms, automation, data analytics, and other technological advancements to streamline processes, increase efficiency, and extend their influence to broader audiences.

c) Replicability and Localization:

Purpose-driven entrepreneurs focus on developing scalable and adaptable models that can be replicated in different contexts. They create frameworks and toolkits that enable their initiatives to be localized and implemented in diverse communities, thus expanding their impact while considering local needs and cultural sensitivities.

18.3 Overcoming Resistance and Generating Awareness:

Purpose-driven entrepreneurs often encounter resistance or lack of awareness about their mission and initiatives. They have employed various strategies to overcome these challenges:

a) Storytelling and Authentic Communication:

Purpose-driven entrepreneurs leverage the power of storytelling to communicate their mission, values, and impact. They use compelling narratives, personal experiences, and real-life examples to engage and inspire others. Authentic communication builds trust and helps create a connection between their audience and the purpose-driven mission.

b) Engaging Stakeholders:

Purpose-driven entrepreneurs actively engage with stakeholders, including customers, employees, community members, and policymakers. They create opportunities for dialogue, listen to feedback, and involve stakeholders in decision-making processes. By fostering meaningful relationships, purpose-driven entrepreneurs build support, generate awareness, and inspire others to join their cause.

c) Advocacy and Thought Leadership:

Purpose-driven entrepreneurs become advocates and thought leaders in their fields. They raise awareness about the social and environmental issues they are addressing, share insights and expertise, and advocate for policy changes that support their mission. By positioning themselves as experts, purpose-driven entrepreneurs gain credibility and influence, creating a platform for wider awareness and impact.

18.4 Sustaining Motivation and Resilience:

Maintaining motivation and resilience is crucial for purpose-driven entrepreneurs, especially during challenging times. They have adopted strategies to stay motivated and overcome setbacks:

a) Finding Support Networks:

Purpose-driven entrepreneurs seek out communities, networks, and mentors who understand their challenges and can provide guidance and support. These networks offer a space for sharing experiences, learning from others, and receiving encouragement during difficult times.

b) Self-Care and Well-being:

Purpose-driven entrepreneurs recognize the importance of self-care and prioritize their well-being. They establish routines that promote physical and mental health, incorporate practices such as meditation or exercise, and create a healthy work-life balance. By taking care of themselves, they can sustain their energy and focus on their purpose-driven mission.

c) Learning from Setbacks:

Purpose-driven entrepreneurs view setbacks as learning opportunities rather than failures. They analyze challenges, identify lessons, and adapt their strategies accordingly. Embracing a growth mindset helps them remain resilient and navigate obstacles with a determination to overcome them.

Purpose-driven entrepreneurs face unique challenges on their journeys to create meaningful impact. By leveraging alternative funding models, embracing collaborative partnerships, and employing effective communication strategies, purpose-driven entrepreneurs overcome financial obstacles, scale their impact, generate awareness, and sustain motivation. Their resilience, innovation, and commitment to their mission inspire others and contribute to a more purpose-driven world.

ᐲᐲᐲ

"Purpose-driven businesses are built on a foundation of trust, authenticity, and a genuine desire to create positive impact."

ᐲᐲᐲ

The Power of Individual Action: Making a Difference as an Employee

How individuals can drive purpose within organizations
Fostering a sense of purpose in the workplace
Practical steps for making a positive impact

ᛈᛈᛈ

NINETEEN

The Power of Individual Action: Making a Difference as an Employee

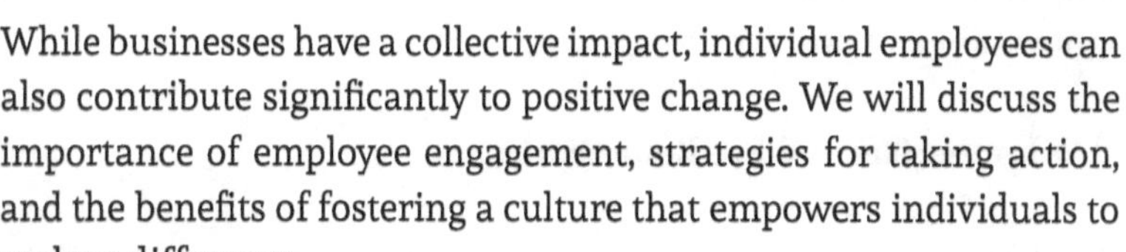

While businesses have a collective impact, individual employees can also contribute significantly to positive change. We will discuss the importance of employee engagement, strategies for taking action, and the benefits of fostering a culture that empowers individuals to make a difference.

19.1 The Importance of Employee Engagement:

Employee engagement is a vital factor in driving positive change within purpose-driven businesses. Engaged employees are more likely to align with the organization's purpose, go the extra mile, and actively contribute to its social and environmental objectives. When employees are engaged, they become agents of change and play a crucial role in creating a positive impact both within the organization and in the wider community.

19.2 Strategies for Taking Action:

Individual employees have various strategies at their disposal to make a difference within their organizations. Here are some key strategies:

a) Embrace and Live the Purpose:

Employees can embrace and embody the purpose and values of the organization in their everyday work. By aligning their actions with the organization's mission, employees contribute to the overall impact and inspire others to do the same.

b) Innovative Problem-Solving:

Employees can proactively identify social and environmental challenges within the organization and propose innovative solutions. By thinking creatively and offering ideas for improvement, individuals contribute to a culture of continuous innovation and positive change.

c) Volunteerism and Pro Bono Work:

Employees can engage in volunteerism or pro bono work that aligns with the organization's purpose. This can involve dedicating time and skills to support nonprofits, community initiatives, or sustainability projects, both individually or as part of corporate volunteering programs.

d) Influence and Collaboration:

Employees can use their influence to drive positive change within their teams and departments. By advocating for sustainable practices, ethical decision-making, and social responsibility, individuals can inspire their colleagues and foster a culture of collective action.

19.3 Benefits of Fostering a Culture of Individual Action:

Fostering a culture that empowers individuals to make a difference has numerous benefits for purpose-driven businesses:

a) Increased Employee Engagement:

When employees feel empowered to contribute to the organization's purpose, their engagement and commitment to their work are enhanced. This leads to improved productivity, higher job satisfaction, and reduced turnover.

b) Enhanced Innovation and Problem-Solving:

Empowering employees to take action fosters a culture of innovation and creative problem-solving. Individuals bring diverse perspectives, ideas, and skills to the table, leading to innovative solutions and continuous improvement.

c) Strengthened Organizational Reputation:

Purpose-driven businesses that support and highlight individual employee action gain a reputation as organizations that prioritize social and environmental impact. This enhances the company's image, attracts top talent, and builds trust among stakeholders.

d) Collective Impact:

When employees are encouraged and empowered to make a difference, their collective actions can drive significant social and environmental impact. By harnessing the power of individual action, purpose-driven businesses can create a ripple effect that extends beyond the organization itself.

19.4 Leadership and Support:

Leadership plays a crucial role in fostering a culture of individual action. Managers and leaders should provide support, resources, and recognition for employees' efforts to make a difference. Key aspects of leadership support include:

a) Clear Communication:

Leaders should communicate the organization's purpose, values, and expectations clearly to employees. This clarity helps individuals understand how their actions can contribute to the organization's mission and encourages them to take initiative.

b) Empowerment and Autonomy:

Leaders should empower employees by providing autonomy and decision-making authority. This autonomy enables individuals to take ownership of their work, identify opportunities for impact, and take action without excessive bureaucracy.

c) Recognition and Rewards:

Leaders should recognize and reward employees' efforts to make a difference. Publicly acknowledging and celebrating individual contributions reinforces a culture of individual action, motivating others to follow suit.

d) Learning and Development:

Leaders should invest in employees' learning and development, providing training opportunities that enhance their skills, knowledge, and understanding of purpose-driven practices. This investment equips individuals with the tools needed to make a meaningful impact.

19.5 Building Networks and Collaboration:

Building networks and fostering collaboration among employees can amplify the impact of individual actions. Encouraging cross-functional collaboration, creating platforms for knowledge-sharing and idea generation, and facilitating connections among employees who share similar interests can lead to synergistic efforts and shared learning. Building strong internal networks strengthens the collective power of individual actions and creates a sense of community within the organization.

Individual employees possess the power to make a difference within purpose-driven businesses. Through employee engagement, innovative problem-solving, volunteerism, and collaboration, individuals contribute to positive change both within the organization and in the wider community. Fostering a culture that empowers individuals to take action has numerous benefits, including increased employee engagement, enhanced innovation, and a strengthened organizational reputation. Leadership support, clear communication, recognition, and learning opportunities are essential in encouraging and supporting individual action. By harnessing the collective power of employees, purpose-driven businesses can amplify their impact and create a culture of positive change."A purpose-driven business is not limited by constraints; it is fueled by the belief that we can change the world."

ৡৡৡ

The Call to Action: Creating a Purpose-Driven Future

The urgency and importance of purpose-driven business
Steps to start or transition towards a purpose-driven organization
Inspiring a movement towards a sustainable and equitable future

ɗɗɗ

TWENTY

THE CALL TO ACTION: CREATING A PURPOSE-DRIVEN FUTURE

We have seen the power and potential of purpose-driven businesses and the positive impact they can have on people and the planet. Now, it's time to take action and work collectively towards building a future that prioritizes purpose, sustainability, and social responsibility.

20.1 Individual Action:

Every individual has a role to play in creating a purpose-driven future. Here are some ways individuals can contribute:

a) Align with Personal Purpose:

Reflect on your own values, passions, and purpose. Identify how you can integrate these into your personal and professional life. By aligning your actions with your purpose, you can make a meaningful difference and inspire others to do the same.

b) Practice Conscious Consumption:

Be mindful of the products and services you choose to support. Consider the social and environmental impact of your purchasing decisions. Support purpose-driven brands and businesses that align with your values.

c) Advocate for Change:

Use your voice to advocate for positive change. Engage in discussions, raise awareness, and support initiatives that address social and environmental challenges. Participate in community events, sign petitions, and connect with like-minded individuals and organizations.

20.2 Business Action:

Businesses play a crucial role in shaping the future. Purpose-driven businesses can lead the way by taking the following actions:

a) Integrate Purpose into Business Strategy:

Embed purpose into the core of your business strategy. Align your mission, values, and operations with social and environmental objectives. Prioritize sustainable practices, responsible sourcing, and ethical decision-making.

b) Foster Collaboration:

Seek out collaboration and partnerships with other purpose-driven businesses, nonprofits, and government agencies. By working together, businesses can leverage their collective strengths, share resources, and drive systemic change.

c) Empower Employees:

Create a culture that empowers employees to make a difference. Foster an environment where individuals are encouraged to take initiative, innovate, and contribute to the organization's purpose. Provide resources, support, and recognition for employee-led initiatives.

20.3 Societal Action:

Creating a purpose-driven future requires collective action at the societal level. Here are some ways society can contribute:

a) Demand Accountability:

Hold businesses and organizations accountable for their social and environmental impact. Advocate for transparent reporting, ethical practices, and responsible behavior. Support regulations and policies that promote sustainability and social responsibility.

b) Educate and Inspire:

Promote education and awareness about purpose-driven practices, sustainability, and social issues. Encourage schools, universities, and community organizations to integrate these topics into curricula and programs. Inspire the next generation to be purpose-driven leaders.

c) Support Social Entrepreneurship:

Foster an ecosystem that supports social entrepreneurs and purpose-driven startups. Provide mentorship, funding, and resources to help them succeed. Recognize and celebrate the contributions of purpose-driven entrepreneurs.

20.4 Collaboration and Partnerships:

Creating a purpose-driven future requires collaboration and partnerships among individuals, businesses, government, and civil society. By working together, we can address complex challenges, share knowledge and resources, and drive meaningful change. Foster relationships based on trust, shared values, and common goals to amplify impact and create a more sustainable and equitable world.

20.5 Continuous Learning and Improvement:

Creating a purpose-driven future is an ongoing journey that requires continuous learning and improvement. Stay informed about emerging trends, best practices, and new technologies that can advance purpose-driven initiatives. Embrace a growth mindset and be open to adapting strategies based on feedback and evaluation.

The call to action is clear: we must collectively create a purpose-driven future that prioritizes sustainability, social responsibility, and positive impact. Individuals, businesses, and society all have roles to play in this transformation. By aligning personal purpose, practicing conscious consumption, advocating for change, integrating purpose into business strategies, fostering collaboration, demanding accountability, supporting social entrepreneurship, and promoting continuous learning, we can build a future that puts people and the planet first. Let us embrace the call to action and work together to create a purpose-driven world for generations to come.

 PPP

"In a purpose-driven business, success is not about conquering; it's about collaboration, compassion, and leaving a lasting legacy."

ᗡᗡᗡ

References And Citations

This book has been created by referencing various websites on the internet, including Wikipedia, in order to gather valuable information and data. In addition to online sources, this book also draws upon the author's own research and includes references to relevant books in the library. By combining a variety of sources, this book provides a comprehensive and well-researched account of the subject matter. The author has taken care to ensure that all information presented is accurate and properly cited to give credit to the original sources.

Although every effort has been made to ensure the accuracy and completeness of the information presented in this book, human errors may still occur. If any reader discovers an error or omission in this book, I respectfully welcome their feedback and encourage them to bring it to my attention. Such feedback is valuable to me, and I will take all necessary steps to correct any errors and improve the content of this book in future editions. Thank you for your understanding and support.

ϼϼϼ

Contact

Dr. Yogendra Singh Yadav
26-MIG, Indira Nagar, Kanpur-26 (Uttar Pradesh - India)
yogendraindiag20@gmail.com

|| LOKAHA SAMASTHAHA SUKHINO BHAVANTU ||

❧❧❧